All About NORTH AMERICAN RACCOONS

Lisa Petrillo

Creating Young Nonfiction Readers

EZ Readers lets children delve into nonfiction at beginning reading levels. Young readers are introduced to new concepts, facts, ideas, and vocabulary.

Tips for Reading Nonfiction with Beginning Readers

Talk about Nonfiction
Begin by explaining that nonfiction books give us information that is true. The book will be organized around a specific topic or idea, and we may learn new facts through reading.

Look at the Parts
Most nonfiction books have helpful features. Our *EZ Readers* include a Contents page, an index, and color photographs. Share the purpose of these features with your reader.

Contents
Located at the front of a book, the Contents displays a list of the big ideas within the book and where to find them.

Index
An index is an alphabetical list of topics and the page numbers where they are found.

Glossary
Located at the back of the book, a glossary contains key words/phrases that are related to the topic.

Photos/Charts
A lot of information can be found by "reading" the charts and photos found within nonfiction text. Help your reader learn more about the different ways information can be displayed.

With a little help and guidance about reading nonfiction, you can feel good about introducing a young reader to the world of *EZ Readers* nonfiction books.

Mitchell Lane
PUBLISHERS

2001 SW 31st Avenue
Hallandale, FL 33009
www.mitchelllanepub.com

Copyright © 2025 by Mitchell Lane Publishers. All rights reserved. No part of this book may be reproduced without written permission from the publisher. Printed and bound in the United States of America.

First Edition, 2025.

Author: Lisa Petrillo
Designer: Ed Morgan
Editor: Sharon F. Doorasamy

Names/credits:
Title: All About North American Raccoons / by Lisa Petrillo
Description: Hallandale, FL : Mitchell Lane Publishers, [2025]

Series: Animals Around the World
Library bound ISBN: 9781680204254
eBook ISBN: 9781680204261
Paperback ISBN: 9798892601399

EZ readers is an imprint of Mitchell Lane Publishers

Library of Congress Cataloging-in-Publication Data
Names: Petrillo, Lisa, author.
Title: All about North American raccoons / by Lisa Petrillo.
Description: First edition. | Hallandale, FL : EZ Readers, an imprint of Mitchell Lane Publishers, 2020. | Series: Animals around the world-North American animals | Includes bibliographical references and index.
Identifiers: LCCN 2018030967| ISBN 9781680204254 (library bound) | ISBN 9781680204261 (ebook)
Subjects: LCSH: Raccoons—Juvenile literature.
Classification: LCC QL737.C26 P49 2020 | DDC 599.76/32—dc23
LC record available at https://lccn.loc.gov/2018030967

Photo credits: Freepik.com, Shutterstock.com, mapchart.net

CONTENTS

Raccoons	**4**
Where Do Raccoons Live?	**22**
Interesting Facts	**23**
Parts of a Raccoon	**23**
Glossary	**24**
Further Reading	**24**
On the Internet	**24**
Index	**24**

Raccoons are found across America. They live in cities, mountains, and even swamps.

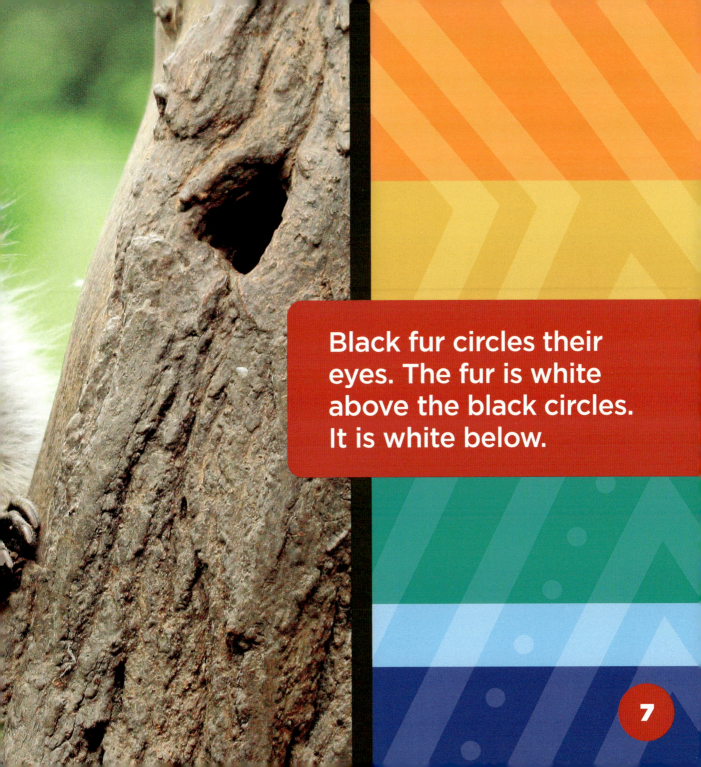

Black fur circles their eyes. The fur is white above the black circles. It is white below.

7

After dark, raccoons **prowl** around. They raid chicken **coops**. They tip over trash.

8

Raccoon tails are bushy with black stripes. The tails are as long as a school ruler. There are five to ten rings per tail.

Raccoons are the size of fat cats. They stand on their back legs to use their front paws.

12

Raccoons eat lots of different foods. They like bugs, toads, and trash.

14

Baby raccoons are called **kits**. Kits live in **dens** with their mothers. They move out when they can hunt.

Raccoons live two to three years. Bobcats, coyotes, and cougars are their enemies. People kill the most raccoons. They hunt them. **Motorists** kill them too.

Raccoons are smart. They climb trees to escape enemies. They swim, too.

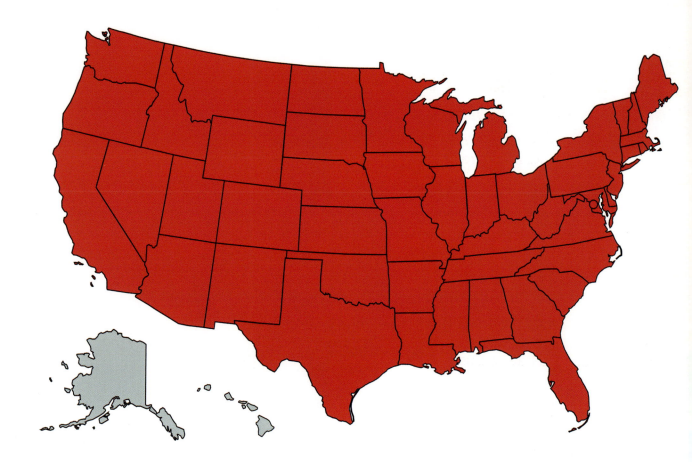

WHERE DO RACCOONS LIVE?

Throughout the United States, except for Alaska and Hawaii.

INTERESTING FACTS

- Raccoon fur is **waterproof** and thick to keep them warm.
- Raccoons talk by clicking their teeth, whistling, snarling, growling, hissing, shrieking, and screaming.
- When a raccoon feels scared, it growls and hunches its rump up even higher.
- Raccoons can open locked doors.

PARTS OF A RACCOON

Tail
Raccoons have a bushy tail that is 8 to 16 inches long.

Paws
Raccoons have five toes on both their front and hind paws.

Ears
The ears of raccoons are in front and slightly rounded, bordered by white fur.

Fur
Raccoons have many mixed colors of gray, white, and brown with black stripes around the tail and face like a mask.

GLOSSARY

coop
A cage for chickens

den
Hollow trees or burrows where raccoons hide their kits

kits
Young raccoons

motorist
Someone who drives a car

prowl
To move slowly and quietly while looking around for prey or food

waterproof
Fur that does not let water through

FURTHER READING

Chenevert, Brian, and Allison A. Gedman. *Azban's Great Journey*. CreateSpace Independent Publishing Platform, 2015.

Hurtig, Jennifer. *Raccoons*. New York: Weigl Publishers, 2008.

Magby, Meryl. *Raccoons*. New York: PowerKids Press, 2014.

Otfinoski, Steven. *Raccoons*. New York: Marshall Cavendish Benchmark, 2011.

Read, Tracy C. *Exploring the World of Raccoons*. Buffalo, NY: Firefly Books, 2010.

ON THE INTERNET

Raccoon: San Diego Zoo
http://animals.sandiegozoo.org/animals/raccoon

Project Wildlife Animals: Raccoons
http://www.projectwildlife.org/animals.php?id=11

8 Facts About Raccoons: CBC Kids
http://www.cbc.ca/kidscbc2/the-feed/8-facts-about-raccoons

Raccoons National Geographic
https://www.nationalgeographic.com/animals/mammals/r/raccoon/

INDEX

America	5
Bobcats	18
Cougars	18
Coyotes	18
Kits	17
Paws	12, 23
Tail	10, 23